Look and Play

Noisy Machines

by Jim Pipe

Aladdin/Watts
London · Sydney

truck

2

A **truck** is noisy.
Rumble!

3

motorbike

A **motorbike** is noisy. Vroom!

4

5

drill

A **drill** is noisy.

lawnmower

A **lawnmower** is noisy.

7

plane

8

A jet **plane** is noisy. Roar!

digger

A **digger** is noisy.
Smash!

11

fire engine

A **fire engine** is noisy.
Weeoh! Weeoh!

13

steam train

14

A **steam train** is noisy. Chuff! Chuff!

15

racing car

16

A **racing car** is noisy. Brrm! Brrm!

helicopter

A **helicopter** is noisy.
Chucka! Chucka!

19

Who am I?

roar!

smash!

rumble!

vroom!

Match the sounds and pictures.

How many?

Can you count the noisy machines? **21**

What noise?

Ship

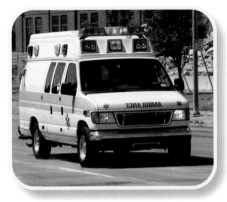

Ambulance

Rocket

Train

Can you sound like these machines?

Index

For Parents and Teachers

Questions you could ask:

p. 2 What other noises might a truck make? Think of a car, e.g. horn, brakes, starting up engine. Throughout the book, encourage the reader to make the noises of the different machines.

p. 4 Can you see the engine? Also point out the exhaust where noise comes out of the engine.

p. 6 What noises do other tools make? e.g. hammer, saw, electric drill, scraper.

p. 8 Are machines noisier when they are close up? Yes – compare the noise from a plane close up, e.g. at an airport, with the noise of a plane high in the sky.

p. 10 What noises do things make when they break? Ask the reader to think about the sounds made by different materials, e.g. wood splintering, glass cracking, plate smashing, clothes ripping.

p. 12 Why does a fire engine have a noisy siren (and flashing lights)? To tell other vehicles to let them through. Ask reader what other vehicles have a siren, e.g. ambulances, police cars/motorbikes.

p. 17 What is that man doing? Holding his hands over his ears to block out the loud sound. The other man is wearing ear muffs for the same reason.

p. 18 What makes the sound on a helicopter? The rotors make a whirring sound as they spin round and round. The rotors lift the helicopter into the air.

Activities you could do:

• Get children to listen to sounds that machines make in classroom, e.g. whirring fan, sound of rolling wheels on hard surface, electric engine in household appliance.

• Role play: ask the reader to act out noises made by machine they are driving, e.g. getting in cab, starting engine, driving along, siren, brakes etc.

• Plan a day for children to bring in toy machines such as planes and diggers and ask them to mimic the noises they make.

• Take children outside to listen for machine noises, e.g. traffic, lawnmower or plane flying overhead.

© Aladdin Books Ltd 2008

Designed and produced by
Aladdin Books Ltd
PO Box 53987
London SW15 2SF

First published in 2008
by Franklin Watts
338 Euston Road
London NW1 3BH

Franklin Watts Australia
Level 17/207 Kent Street
Sydney, NSW 2000

All rights reserved
Printed in Malaysia

A catalogue record for this book is available from the British Library.

Dewey Classification:
621.8

ISBN 978 0 7496 8620 8

Franklin Watts is a division of Hachette Children's Books, an Hachette Livre UK company.
www.hachettelivre.co.uk

Series consultant
Zoe Stillwell is an experienced Early Years teacher currently teaching at Pewley Down Infant School, Guildford.

Photocredits:
l-left, r-right, b-bottom, t-top, c-centre, m-middle
All photos from istockphoto.com except: 2-3, 20tl, 23br – Courtesy Mack Trucks, Inc. 22bl – Corbis.